200 Sight W

a	cut	has	not	six	warm
about	could	have	now	sleep	was
after	come	he	of	small	wash
again	did	help	off	so	we
all	do	her	old	some	well
always	does	here	on	soon	went
am	don't	him	once	stop	were
an	done	his	one	take	what
and	down	how	open	tell	when
any	draw	I	or	ten	where
are	drink	in	our	thank	which
around	eat	into	out	that	white
as	eight	it	over	the	who
ask	every	it's	own	their	why
at	fast	jump	play	them	will
ate	find	just	please	then	wish
away	first	keep	push	there	with
be	five	know	pull	these	work
because	fly	let	put	they	would
been	for	like	ran	think	write
before	found	little	read	this	yellow
best	four	live	red	those	yes
big	from	look	ride	three	you
black	full	made	right	to	your
blue	funny	make	round	today	
both	gave	many	run	too	
bring	get	may	said	try	
brown	give	me	saw	two	
but	go	much	say	under	
by	goes	most	see	up	
call	going	my	seven	us	
came	good	never	she	use	
can	got	new	show	very	
clean	grow	nine	sing	walk	
cold	had	no	sit	want	

Practice Sentences

Fill in the feature word in each sentence.

1 I'm done my homework.

2 Make a wish.

3 I gave her a hug.

4 Please sit over there.

5 You can read.

6 We went to the store.

7 I saw an airplane.

8 They met in school.

GOOD JOB!

Practice Sentences

Fill in the feature word in each sentence.

1 Flowers grow in the garden.

2 Are we there yet?

3 This is how we play.

4 Please open the door.

5 We are best friends.

6 Time to go outside.

7 I ran by the park.

8 I love to eat pizza.

9 Let me think.

10 How does this work?

GOOD JOB!

Practice Sentences

Fill in the feature word in each sentence.

1. Time to find my shoes.

2. The ball is round.

3. I have one apple.

4. Bring it to me.

5. Not this time.

6. I own a pencil.

7. This is our house.

8. I love to but not right now.

9. My dad said hello.

10. I will ask the teacher.

GOOD JOB!

Practice Sentences

Fill in the feature word in each sentence.

1 The bus is full of kids.

2 Time to get to work.

3 I ate most of my dinner.

4 This is my right hand.

5 Let me show you how.

6 That was her favorite pet.

7 My mom said yes.

8 The dog was nice to me.

9 I was happy today.

10 I had a good day.

GOOD JOB!

Practice Sentences

Fill in the feature word in each sentence.

1 I ate all of my lunch.

2 This is my bike.

3 I will show you where to go.

4 We could dance together.

5 I am proud of myself.

6 They like books.

7 She came to school today.

8 The cat slept for an hour.

9 I like to read.

10 I did my chores.

GOOD JOB!

Practice Sentences

Fill in the feature word in each sentence.

1 My mom has a big heart.

2 The dog has four legs.

3 I live with my parents.

4 Please and thank you.

5 I`ll try again.

6 Who are you?

7 I woke up at ten o`clock.

8 I learned about space.

9 My grandma is old.

10 I want a new toy.

Practice Sentences

Fill in the feature word in each sentence.

1. I like to draw on paper.

2. The won both games.

3. This is new to us.

4. They have pets.

5. Put your boots on.

6. He is a singer.

7. I like red and blue.

8. The baby was very little.

9. The game is over.

10. I played with my toy.

GOOD JOB!

Practice Sentences

Fill in the feature word in each sentence.

1. I can jump high.
2. I see a bird.
3. This is so much fun.
4. When did you last see him?
5. Turn around.
6. I don't feel very well.
7. My blanket is warm.
8. The party will be indoors.
9. They play once a week.
10. The truck is yellow.

GOOD JOB!

Practice Sentences

Fill in the feature word in each sentence.

1 She has been tired lately.

2 Turn off the light.

3 I waited all day.

4 My mom made soup.

5 I will go to the store.

6 Your hair looks nice.

7 Let`s go out to eat.

8 The car came to a stop.

9 We can stay.

10 He is very lucky.

GOOD JOB!

Practice Sentences

Fill in the feature word in each sentence.

1. His shoes are blue.

2. He put away his toys.

3. I gave it to them.

4. What time is it?

5. I went up the stairs.

6. I will call my friend.

7. It was cold outside.

8. I don't want any dessert.

9. My ball is red.

10. The baby is so small.

GOOD JOB!

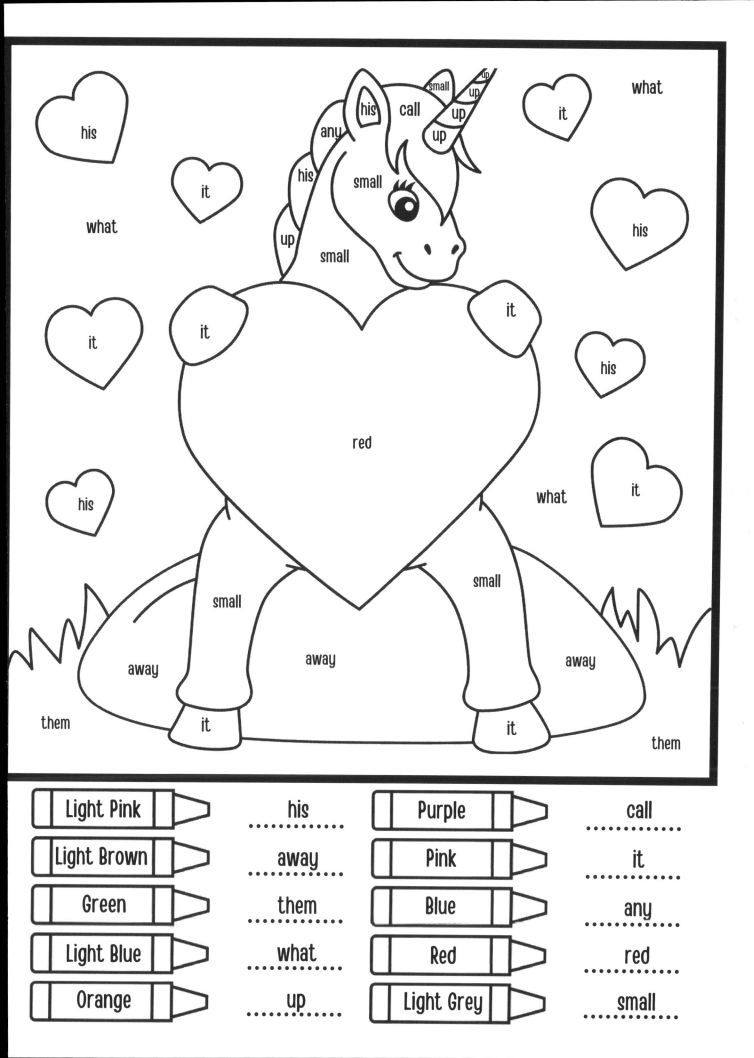

Practice Sentences

Fill in the feature word in each sentence.

1 Slow as a snail.

2 The dog goes outside.

3 The movie was funny.

4 I am three years old.

5 She was very sad.

6 We were very excited.

7 I want to learn to fly.

8 Thank you.

9 No more cookies.

10 My feet are cold.

Practice Sentences

Fill in the feature word in each sentence.

1. Look at that sign.

2. I cut paper.

3. My dog is the best.

4. Come here now.

5. Why are you sad?

6. I have four brothers.

7. My favorite color is blue.

8. Pull the rope.

9. Only take one.

10. I love you so much.

GOOD JOB!

Practice Sentences

Fill in the feature word in each sentence.

1. Dessert is after dinner.

2. I have six crayons.

3. I like playing soccer too.

4. He got a present.

5. She fell down.

6. He will make a craft.

7. I use my tooth brush.

8. It is warm outside.

9. The dog likes to run.

10. We may be late.

GOOD JOB!

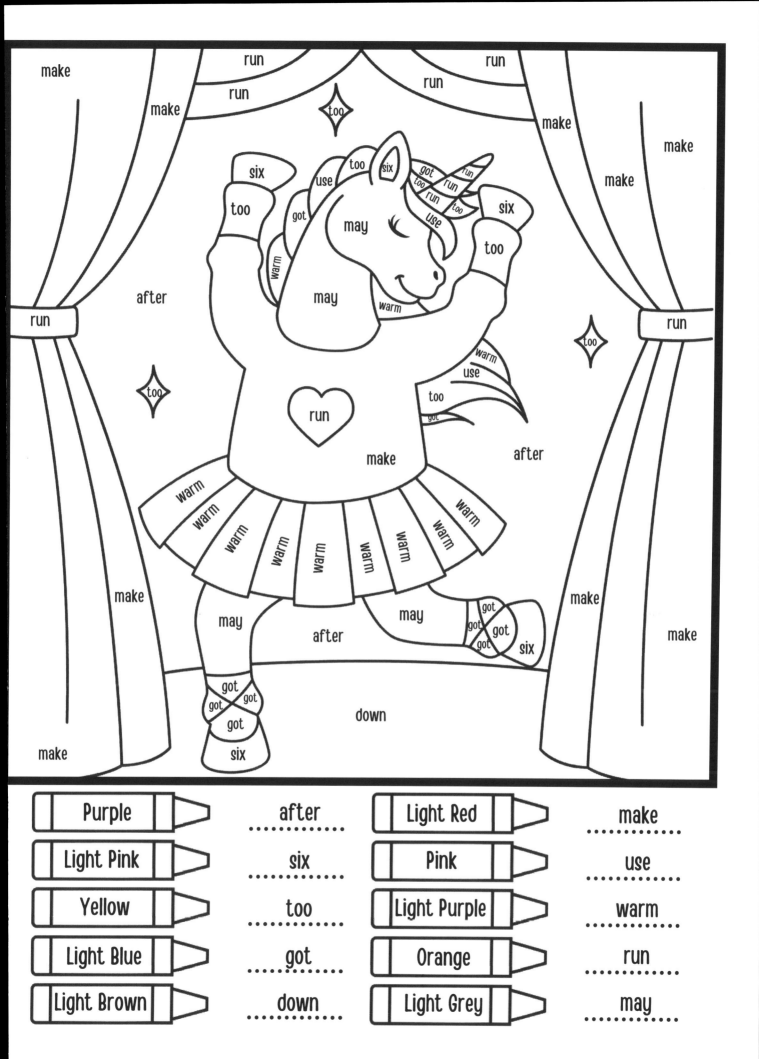

Practice Sentences

Fill in the feature word in each sentence.

1 The race car is fast.

2 He loves lions.

3 Those are my gloves.

4 I walk my dog.

5 He took care of his sister.

6 I will go to school soon.

7 I will do my best.

8 I got a new bike.

9 We are going home.

10 Come over here.

GOOD JOB!

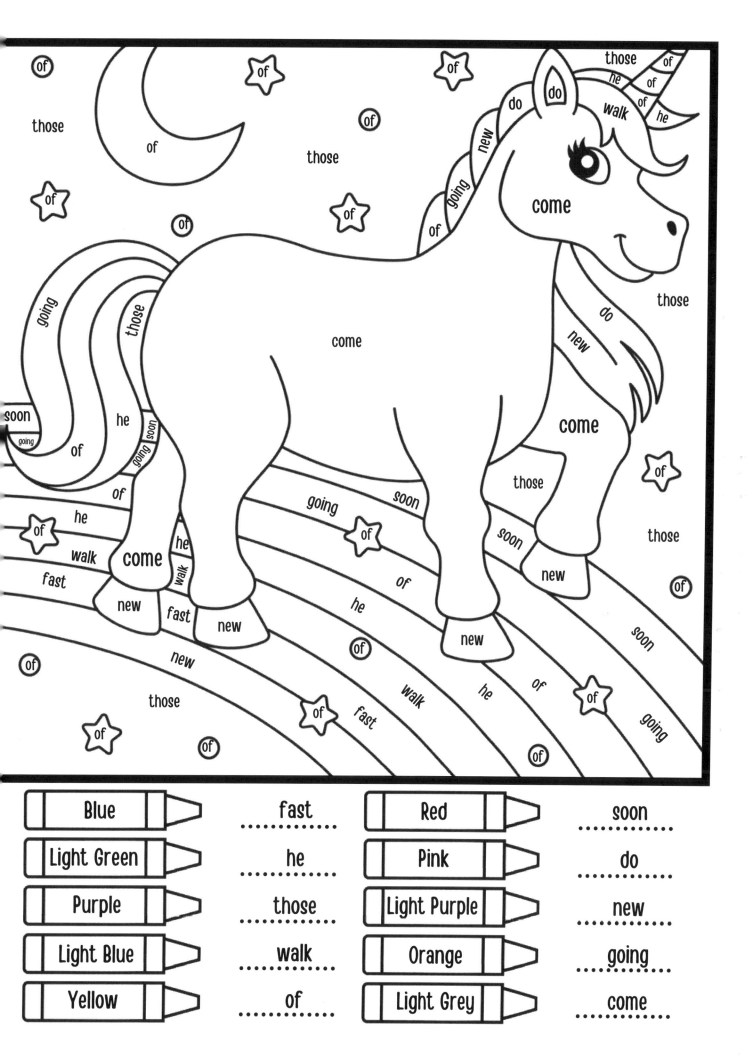

Practice Sentences

Fill in the feature word in each sentence.

1 I don`t know answer.

2 There is so many bugs.

3 The girls love to sing.

4 I fell at the park.

5 Here is my plate.

6 I have two pillows.

7 I like to give hugs.

8 Red or blue?

9 Just help yourselves.

10 My brother is nine.

GOOD JOB!

Practice Sentences

Fill in the feature word in each sentence.

1. Lets play again.
2. I saw an airplane.
3. I like to bake.
4. I will take care of him.
5. He put on his socks.
6. Chores are hard work.
7. She likes to ride her horse.
8. I cried because I fell down.

GOOD JOB!

Practice Sentences

Fill in the feature word in each sentence.

1 Can I have some more ?

2 Keep your things safe.

3 The cat ran away.

4 I will help my mom.

5 That is my favorite drink .

6 Time to clean up.

7 Don`t look down.

8 The sky is so beautiful.

9 Tell the truth.

10 Let`s sit down.

Practice Sentences

Fill in the feature word in each sentence.

1. Wash your hands.

2. I am silly.

3. I see a rainbow.

4. Please have some more.

5. He had a sore tooth.

6. Put your toys in the bin.

7. She needs more sleep.

8. The dog ran to the door.

9. I can read a book.

10. I play every day.

GOOD JOB!

Practice Sentences

Fill in the feature word in each sentence.

1 This is my bike.

2 I let him play with my toy.

3 She put on her mittens.

4 I can say the alphabet.

5 He went to the pool today.

6 Please use your fork.

7 I`ll see you then.

8 I was very hungry.

9 I gave him a ball.

10 Cats can jump high.

Practice Sentences

Fill in the feature word in each sentence.

1. Today is my birthday.

2. Let's ask the teacher.

3. He likes to play games.

4. She did her homework.

5. It's their house.

6. I can write my name.

7. Let me show you how.

8. I ate an apple.

GOOD JOB!

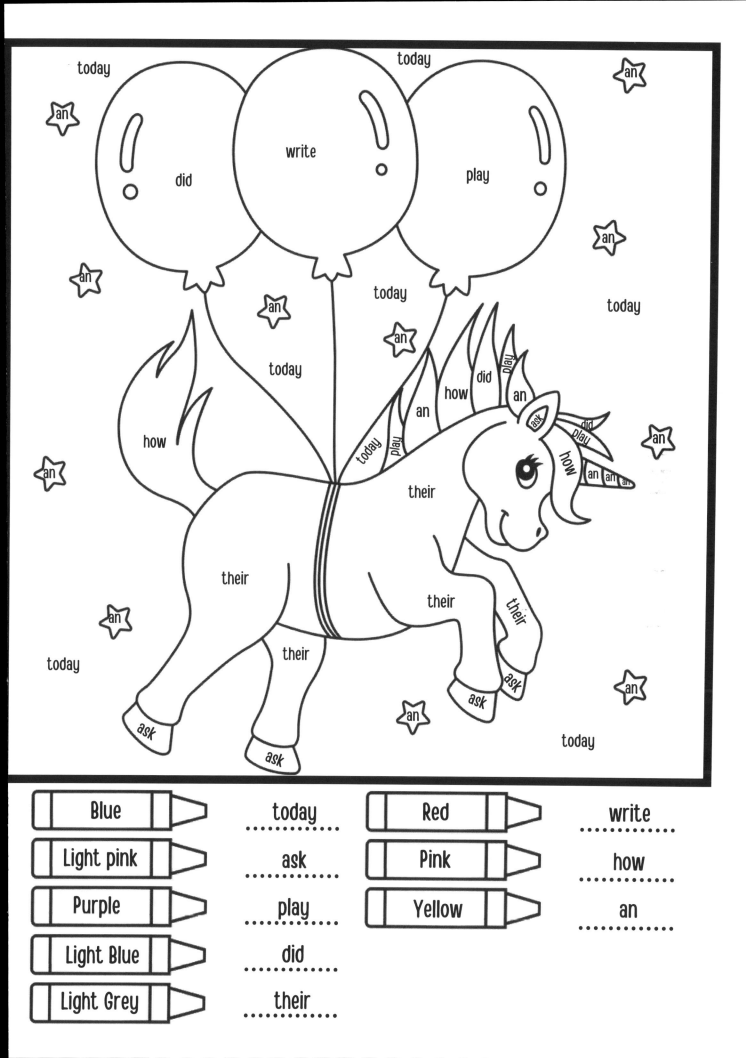

Practice Sentences

Fill in the feature word in each sentence.

1. The dog licked me.

2. This is our car.

3. She came into the room.

4. He always tries very hard.

5. My hair is brown.

6. The tree was very tall.

7. The cat is under the table.

8. Look at the kitten's nose.

9. This is my shirt.

10. We are having fun.

GOOD JOB!

Practice Sentences

Fill in the feature word in each sentence.

1 She gave it to him.

2 The school is far from here.

3 I got a lot of mail today.

4 Spiders have eight legs.

5 I have five rubber balls.

6 He did a cartwheel.

7 Thank you so much.

8 I can't eat any more.

9 Her hair is pretty.

10 I ran to the store.

Practice Sentences

Fill in the feature word in each sentence.

1 I ate too much dessert.

2 Try your best.

3 Ask a question.

4 I have never been on a bus.

5 The car's tires are black.

6 The sun is bright.

7 I call my Dad every day.

8 Please put your toys away.

9 I'm done coloring.

10 I was first in the race.

GOOD JOB!

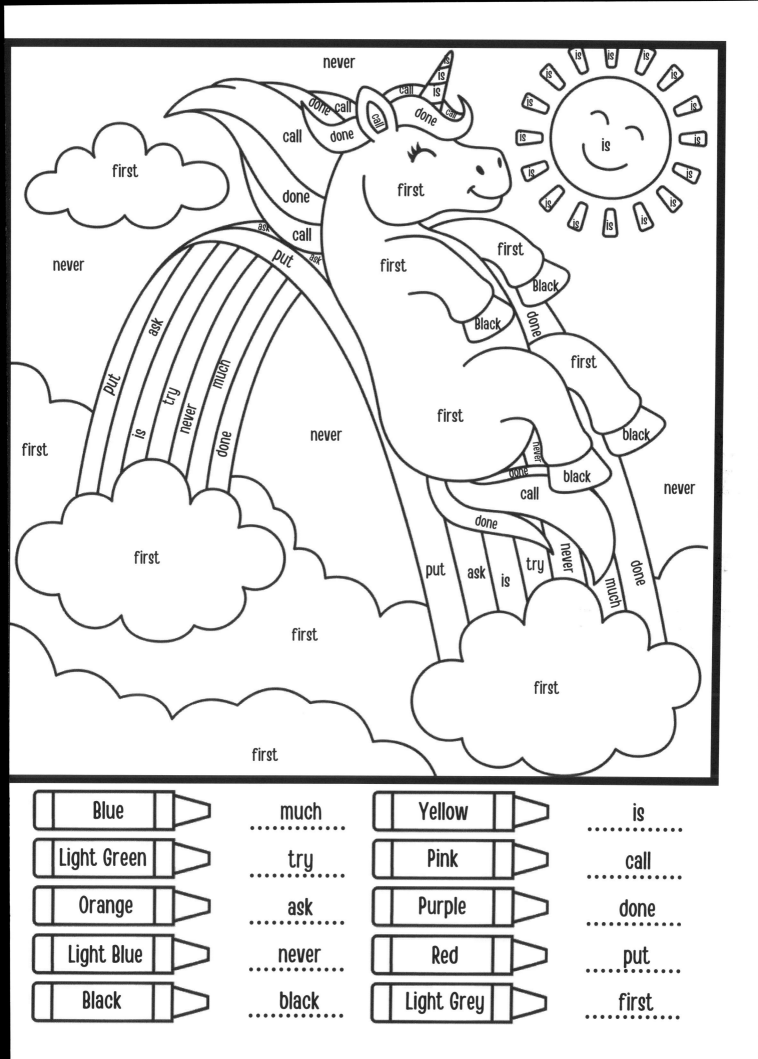

Practice Sentences

Fill in the feature word in each sentence.

1 We had so much fun.

2 You'll grow into it.

3 It may snow today.

4 These socks do not match.

5 You are my best friend.

6 Be careful said mom.

7 I've read that book before.

8 Time to take a break.

9 I will go to bed early.

10 I can count to ten.

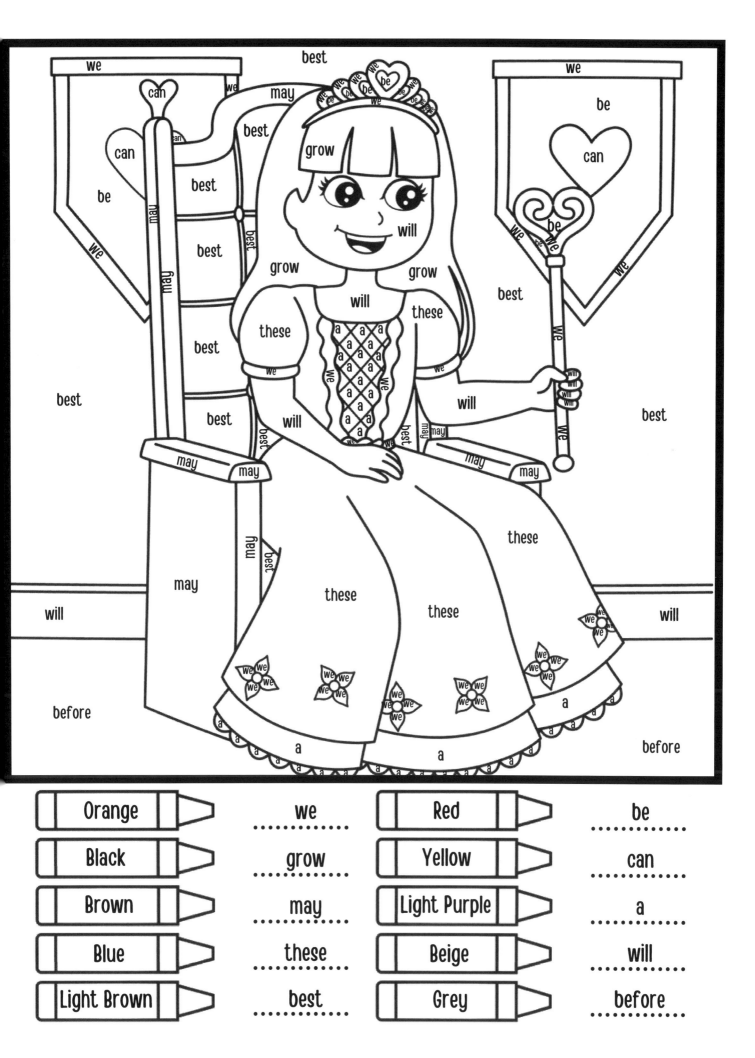

Practice Sentences

Fill in the feature word in each sentence.

1. I found my teddy bear.
2. Eat your vegetables.
3. No one told me that.
4. You look so pretty.
5. Which one should I pick?
6. There goes my sister.
7. Rise and shine.
8. He was very happy.
9. I caught a cold.
10. She loves to sing.

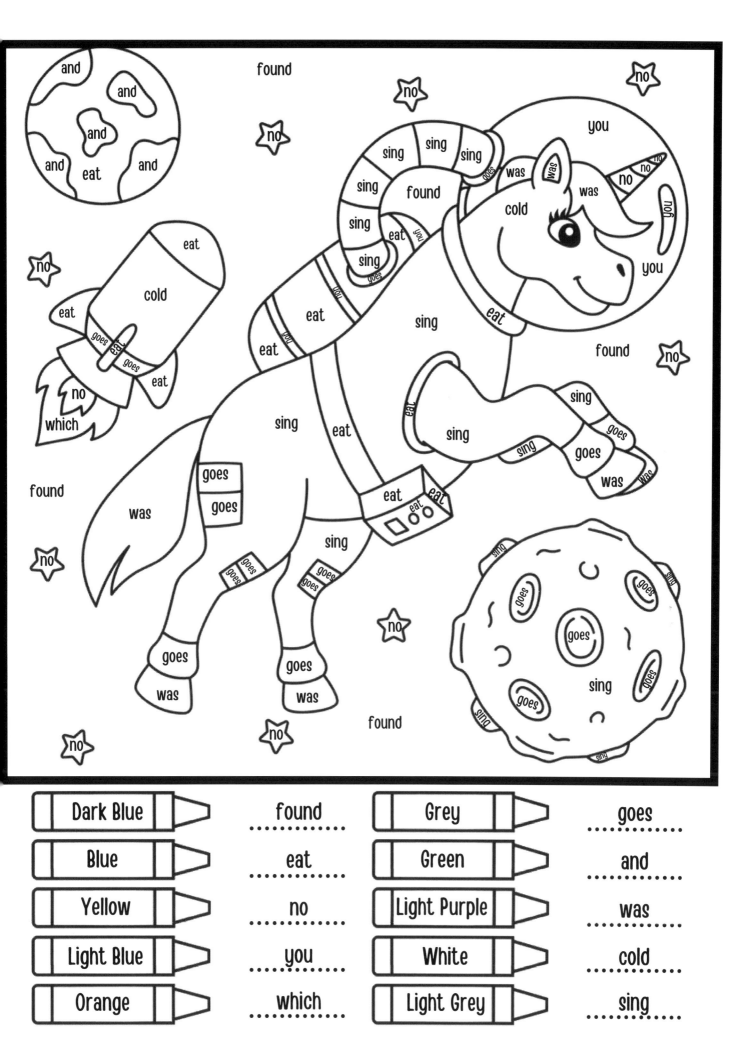

Practice Sentences

Fill in the feature word in each sentence.

1. The paper is white.

2. Now it's your turn.

3. You've been very good.

4. Thanks so much.

5. Time to get started.

6. I can't find my toy.

7. There is a lion at the zoo.

8. She has nice smile.

9. We're out of ideas.

10. My mom loves us.

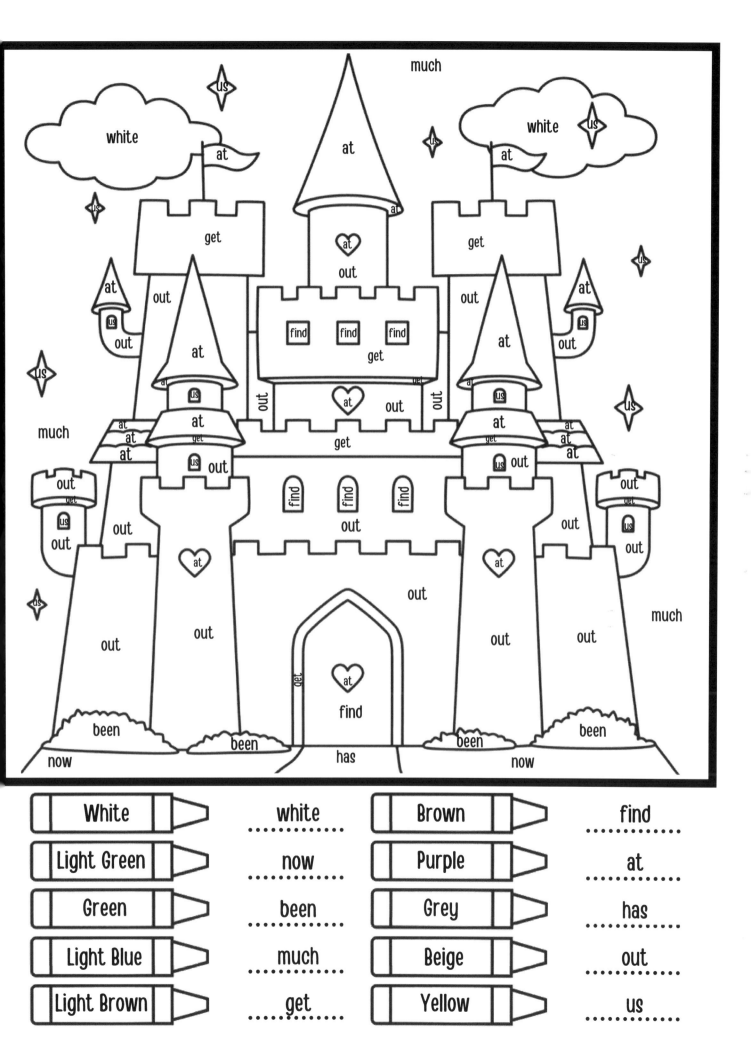

Practice Sentences

Fill in the feature word in each sentence.

1. You did well on your test.

2. I like chocolate too.

3. I'm new here.

4. We played with a ball.

5. Wait here please.

6. My hat is red.

7. He put on a blue jacket.

8. I like my teacher.

9. How was the movie?

10. We both like cars.

GOOD JOB!

Practice Sentences

Fill in the feature word in each sentence.

1. They took away my toy.

2. He ran as fast as he could.

3. Birds can fly .

4. I made dinner.

5. We took a ride on a train.

6. I had the best day.

7. Can you ask for help?

8. Her doll was very special.

9. I have many books.

10. This is fun.

Practice Sentences

Fill in the feature word in each sentence.

1. They talk too much.

2. The plane flew by.

3. Done just in time.

4. They can see us.

5. I don`t know the answer.

6. We sang as we walked.

7. They gave it to me.

8. I was very tired.

9. Our house is small.

10. I`ll be back soon.

Practice Sentences

Fill in the feature word in each sentence.

1 You should not give up.

2 They go to my school.

3 I read a book every day.

4 He jumped into the water.

5 I am smart.

6 She cut the watermelon.

7 It's cold in here.

8 I enjoyed the show.

9 I took my shoes off.

10 Look in the box.

Practice Sentences

Fill in the feature word in each sentence.

1 Both of us like soccer.

2 We have four dogs.

3 I slept very well.

4 I gave it to them.

5 He invited me to a party.

6 We don`t have any apples.

7 I have a gift to give you.

8 Please sit down.

9 Let`s go out to eat.

10 I saw a rabbit.

Practice Sentences

Fill in the feature word in each sentence.

1 I do love this game.

2 He got a new sweater.

3 I saw her this morning.

4 He is very kind.

5 I'm feeling fine now.

6 She has so many toys.

7 Put it back.

8 Mom said time for dinner.

9 We went to the zoo.

10 I'm very hungry.

GOOD JOB!

Practice Sentences

Fill in the feature word in each sentence.

1 The phone was easy to use.

2 What time is it?

3 We went for a walk.

4 I'm going to make a cake.

5 I'll see you tomorrow.

6 I use an umbrella.

7 Call me back.

8 I like to draw hearts.

9 The kids are home.

10 I gave him a ride.

GOOD JOB!

Practice Sentences

Fill in the feature word in each sentence.

1. It's pretty sunny today.

2. Time to say goodbye.

3. He was full of surprises.

4. You can bring your toy.

5. The dogs are playing.

6. She is a friend of mine.

7. We sat by a warm fire.

8. She likes to run.

9. Give me time to think.

10. Thanks so much.

GOOD JOB!

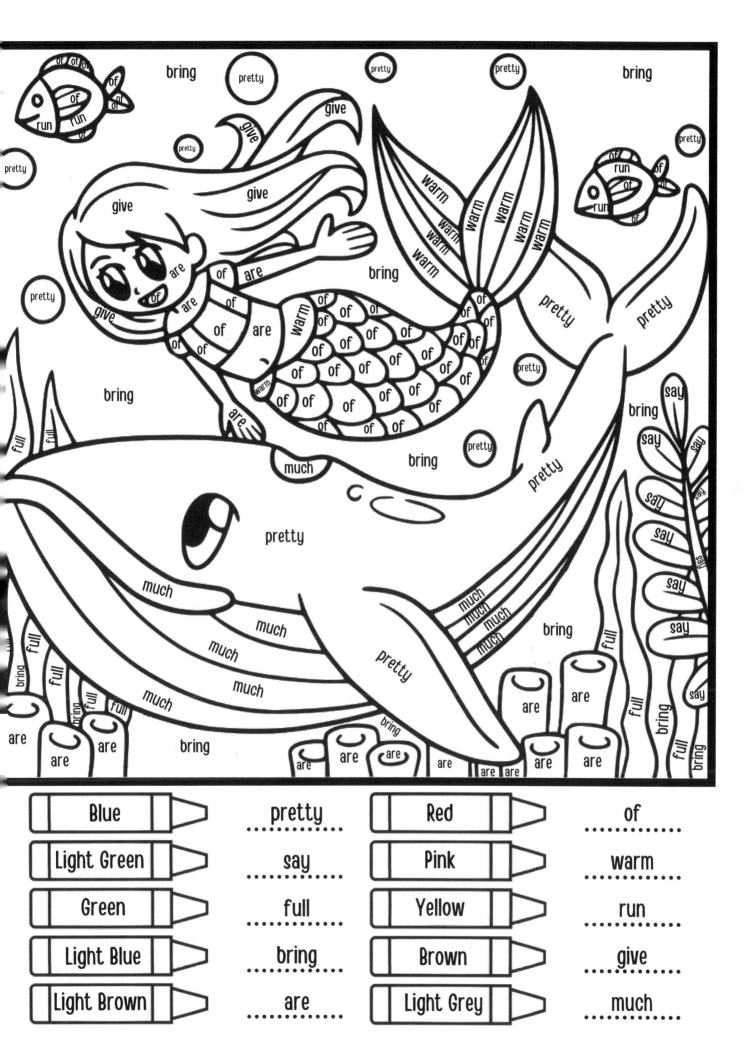

Practice Sentences

Fill in the feature word in each sentence.

1 Every day is a gift.

2 Please do your chores.

3 I`m tired, but I can`t sleep.

4 He will go swimming.

5 She is my sister.

6 The birds like to sing.

7 I got home at seven.

8 I`m here to help you.

9 Time to get up.

10 I ate an apple.

Practice Sentences

Fill in the feature word in each sentence.

1. Time to go to school.

2. I don't have any money.

3. I gave him a present.

4. I have to go to bed.

5. She has three sisters.

6. Today is my birthday.

7. They all grow up.

8. I live here.

9. Why is the sky blue?

Practice Sentences

Fill in the feature word in each sentence.

1 The box is brown.

2 Come sit right next to me.

3 There goes the dog.

4 I need to use the phone.

5 He is my brother.

6 I can ride a bike.

7 Please say hello.

8 They are nice people.

9 Who are you?

10 I found my gloves.

GOOD JOB!

Practice Sentences

Fill in the feature word in each sentence.

1 I ate too much .

2 We are good friends.

3 The answer is yes or no.

4 I`ve seen her before .

5 Let me read the paper.

6 Cookies or icecream?

7 That would be fun.

8 I ate a banana.

9 Come along with us .

GOOD JOB!

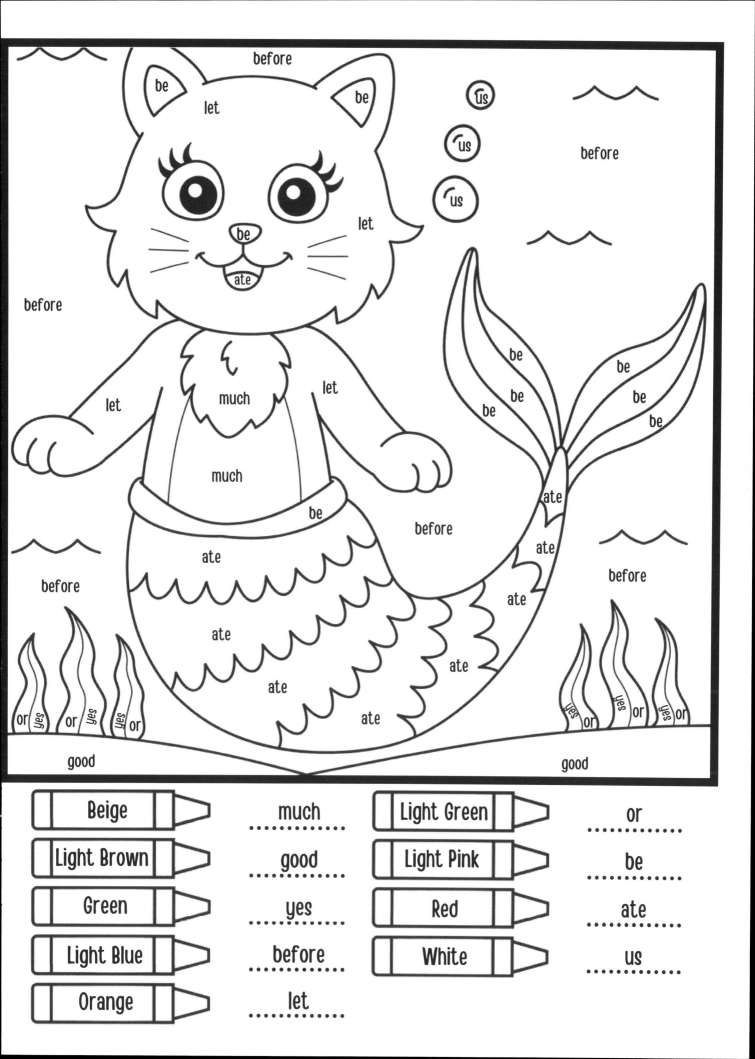

Practice Sentences

Fill in the feature word in each sentence.

1. They are about to leave.

2. Please bring me a cup.

3. The bus drove by.

4. I'm done my homework.

5. I'm five years old.

6. Sit by me.

7. She poured the tea out.

8. Would you like dessert?

9. I like to play outside.

10. I have two legs.

GOOD JOB!

Practice Sentences

Fill in the feature word in each sentence.

1 Please come again.

2 You are my hero.

3 It was a very big room.

4 The little child was lost.

5 I am a boy.

6 I am so excited.

7 That was so funny.

8 I have just eaten lunch.

9 She did her best.

10 I have been busy.

GOOD JOB!

Practice Sentences

Fill in the feature word in each sentence.

1. Come with us.

2. She did well on her test.

3. I found my pen.

4. He got a new hat.

5. My mom said yes.

6. I have ten dollars.

7. He does the dishes.

8. I like to walk in the park.

9. This made him happy.

GOOD JOB!

Practice Sentences

Fill in the feature word in each sentence.

1 Take a look around.

2 She always wears pink.

3 Come to my house.

4 Do you have any fruit?

5 The day went by fast.

6 I love you so much.

7 She had a good day.

8 This is an egg.

9 Go to sleep.

10 This table isn't clean.

GOOD JOB!

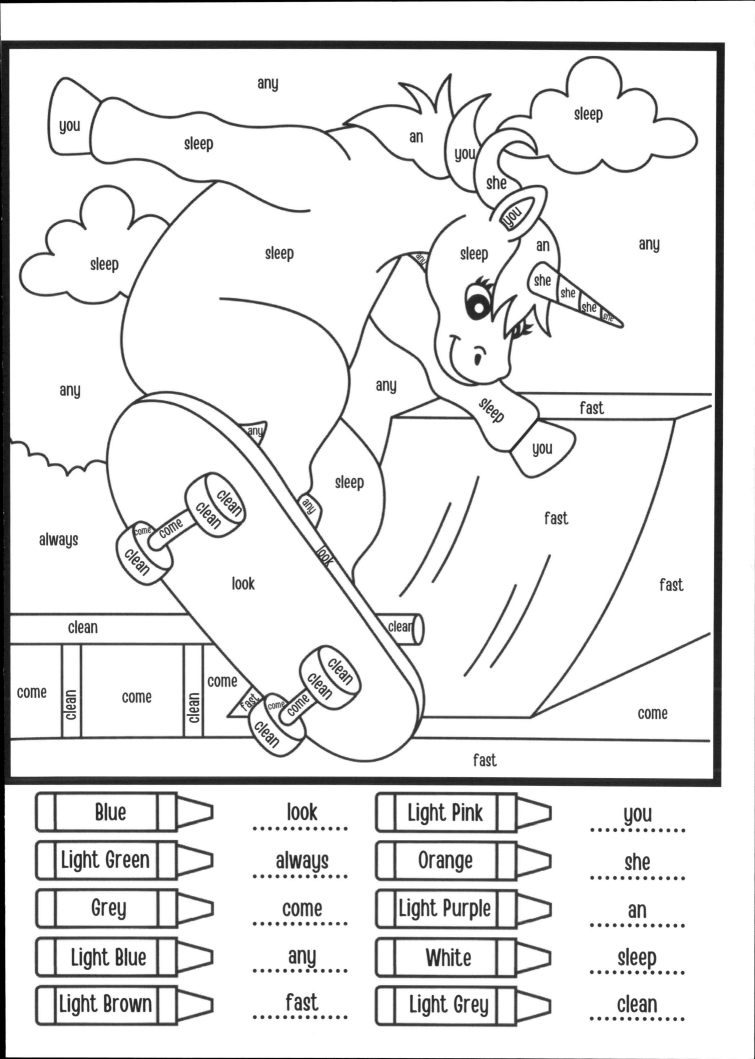

Practice Sentences

Fill in the feature word in each sentence.

1 We don`t have any milk.

2 I will go there tomorrow.

3 Turn right then left.

4 This is my book.

5 I like music.

6 He wants to be a doctor.

7 It must be really cold out.

8 They went inside.

9 She gave it to him.

10 He fell down.

GOOD JOB!

Practice Sentences

Fill in the feature word in each sentence.

1 I gave it to him.

2 In or out?

3 The soup is too hot.

4 We sang as we walked.

5 I want to surprise her.

6 I have a daughter and son.

7 She made a phone call.

GOOD JOB!

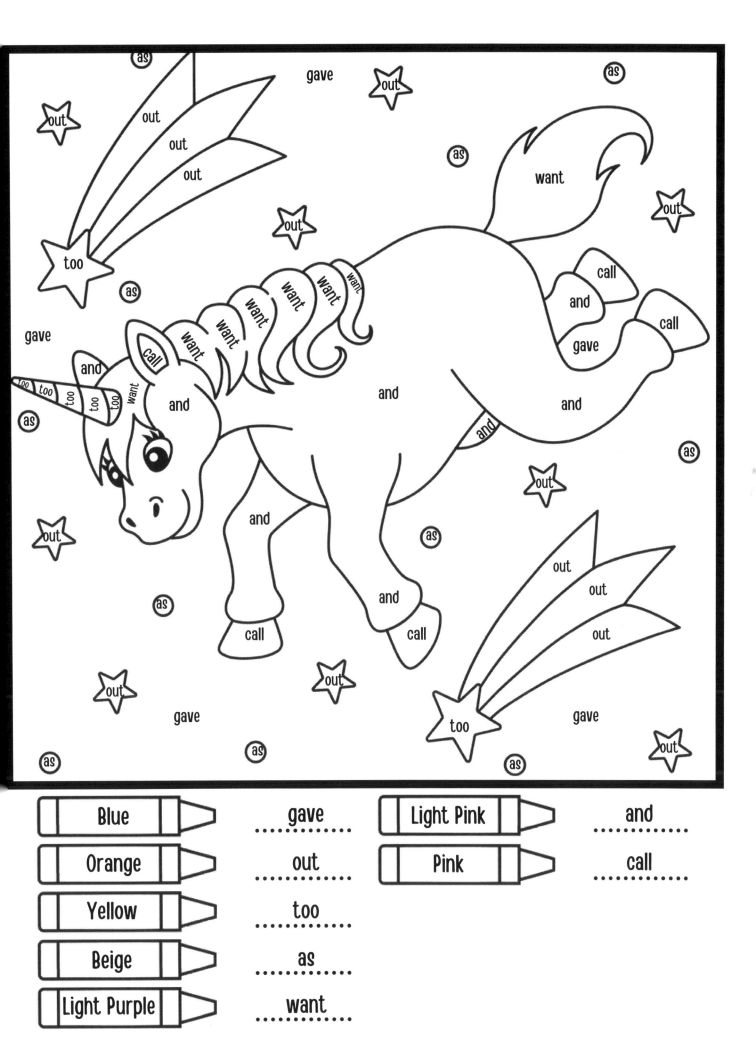

Practice Sentences

Fill in the feature word in each sentence.

1   I saw the moon in the sky.

2   Please stay here.

3   She made dinner.

4   This is where I live.

5   All my friends were there.

6   I have got to go now.

7   This book is old.

8   I was out all day.

9   He got a cold.

10 I saw a pig.

GOOD JOB!

Practice Sentences

Fill in the feature word in each sentence.

1. She has nine pens.

2. He went with her.

3. Pull as hard as you can.

4. Just give him your pencil.

5. Please help your sister.

6. I hope you will join us .

7. Do no run too fast.

8. You are so funny.

9. The clock stopped.

10. I think that it is good.

GOOD JOB!

Made in the USA
Middletown, DE
29 November 2023

44002866R00053